HOW TO EAT IN ITALY

...IF CHICKEN PARM IS YOUR FAVORITE ITALIAN DISH

Carol Coviello-Malzone

Copyright © 2012 Carol Coviello-Malzone

All rights reserved. No part of this story may be used or reproduced in any manner without written permission from the author, except in the case of quotations used in articles and reviews.

ISBN: 978-0-578-11108-7

All photography by Carol Coviello-Malzone

Design by www.marketingintelligently.com
Front cover photograph: © Stokkete | Dreamstime.com

The views expressed in this book are solely those of the author.

For more information, please visit:
www.flavorsofrome.com

To my mother, grandmothers, and aunts who placed wonderful food in front of me and gave an eight year-old child the palate of a crusty gourmand.

And to my many culinary mentors in Italy who later took my lust for food and showed me the art of eating in Italy, meal by amazing meal.

This book is for you if:

You're going to Italy and plan to eat.

You grew up in an Italian family outside of the Old Country.

You lived next door to an Italian family who force fed you every time your walked in the door.

You've eaten in Italian restaurants in any of the 50 States, mostly chains and particularly those playing Italian language tapes in the bathrooms.

You can't wait to get to Italy to have "real" chicken parm.

HOW TO EAT IN ITALY

...IF CHICKEN PARM IS YOUR FAVORITE ITALIAN DISH

Eating in Italy is an art form as revered by the Italians as the sculptures of Michelangelo, the operas of Verdi, and the vocal chords of the late Pavarotti, all of whom were rumored to have enjoyed a good plate of pasta. Eating in Italy can also be a life changing experience for the tourist.

But if your Italian travel fantasies involve dining on spaghetti and meatballs, manicotti, or the world's best chicken parm, such expectations, like searching for the meaning of life, can lead to a big letdown. Those iconic Italian-American dishes haven't disappeared from the Italian table over time, they were never there in the first place.

Italian food as we know it in the U.S. is a hybrid cuisine, one born from the recipes and memories carried to our shores over 100 years ago on the backs of the mostly Southern Italians and Sicilians escaping a land that offered no better future than starvation, poverty, and hardship. After a long ocean voyage, those early 20th century immigrants couldn't get away from Ellis Island fast enough to set up their new kitchens and start feeding their families-as well as the rest of the surrounding area. Not a stroll in the piazza, as they soon discovered.

Life was different on this side of the Atlantic, and along the journey from immigration to assimilation, an entirely new cuisine was born. Because of a lack of some products and the availability of others, a shift in methods and a change in recipes occurred, subtle at first, but becoming more noticeable as the first generation born in this country began setting up their own kitchens.

After World War II, the children of those courageous immigrants found themselves higher up on the economic ladder, and what better way to flaunt this upward mobility than at the table. Portions became larger, sauces became thicker, and entire dishes never known in the old country became part of our daily menus—spaghetti and meatballs, manicotti, and chicken parm.

By the mid-1950's, every American of every ethnic origin could eat Italian. Thanks to a chef from southern Italy by the name of Ettore Boiardi (aka Chef Boyardee), our grocery store shelves were well-stocked with cans of ravioli, spaghettiOs, and beefaroni, the perfect food over which to shake and shake and shake that green container of grated parmesan--which we later found out was no relation at all to Parmigiano-Reggiano.

Thus was a culinary tradition established. This newly created "Italian" menu (whose roster of classic dishes also includes baked ziti, sausages and peppers, and wedding soup) became a bonding agent for family gatherings and eventually set a standard for what Americans imagined Italians were eating in the ancestral homeland. And it's what many of us expect when we travel to Italy for the first time.

The evolution of the Italian-American food plan has been on a roll ever since. In the 1970's and '80's, another layer of well-intentioned misinformation was added to the mix when a contingent of restaurateurs and chefs from various regions of Italy arrived on the American culinary landscape introducing us to fettuccine Alfredo, chicken marsala, and a variety of "refined" non-red sauce dishes which came to be thought of - mistakenly - as Northern Italian cuisine. The recipes generally were the result of poetic license taken by these transplanted cooks to satisfy the American palate and not at all what Italians were eating on the shores of the Mediterranean. Even today's TV celebrity chefs rarely offer up the real deal. What goes on in the kitchens of Italy is often lost in translation over here.

So if eating in Italy is nothing like the menu at Carrabba's, what's the hungry tourist to do? You forget everything you thought you knew about Italian food, learn some basic rules, pull up a chair, ...and eat as the Italians do.

WHAT YOU SHOULD KNOW TO EAT LIKE A NATIVE

...OR AT LEAST AN INFORMED TOURIST

THERE IS NO MASON-DIXON LINE IN ITALY
...and there's no such thing as Northern and Southern Italian food.

Italia omnis est divisa in partes viginti which, to paraphrase Julius Caesar's account of Gaul that many of us read in Latin class, means Italy is a country divided into 20 parts, and each of these parts, or regions as they're called, has its own distinct cuisine determined by geography, history, and tradition.

It wasn't until 1861 that the fragmented European peninsula merged to become the unified country of Italy, with every region clinging for dear life to its individuality. Nowhere is this fierce attachment to place more evident than at the table.

Because the genetic makeup of every Italian in every region determined the need for good food and because historically times were often tough, they learned to create edible masterpieces from the material outside their front door, from the land and sea provisions of nature. And nature provided plenty!

As an example, the cold weather comfort dish of *fonduta* (creamy melted fontina cheese with shaved white truffles into which you dip crusty bread) originated in the Alpine climate of the Val D'Osta. The Chianina cattle grazing under the sun of Tuscany — and nowhere else in Italy — provides *bistecca alla fiorentina* (grilled porterhouse steak), famous in and around Florence. And because something in the moist earth surrounding Rome produces artichokes like nowhere else on earth, *carciofi alla giudia* (artichokes flash-fried to golden delicate crispiness and ending up like golden chrysanthemums on the plate) is a *must-eat* in The Eternal City.

Remember this when traveling from region to region: not only is there a change of hotel rooms, there's also a change of menu. If you fall in love with *risi e bisi* (roughly rice and peas soup) in Venice, don't ask for it in Naples. You won't find it. And if you do, it will have been made grudgingly by the Neapolitans who want you to order *gnocchi alla sorrentina* (potato dumplings covered with tomato sauce and *scamorza* cheese). That's what they eat in Naples and that's what you should eat when you're in their city. So be a locavore in Italy and you'll always eat well!

This fierce sense of pride of place, *campanilismo* as it's referred to in Italy, is a good thing. It's what makes Italian food the best cuisine in the world, and it's what will have you forever longing for that delectable *pasta di pesce spada* (pasta with swordfish and tomato sauce) - as it can only be had in Sicily - long after you've settled into the routine of life back home.

CAVEAT #1:
Don't stress about memorizing all the regional specialities before leaving on your trip. Simply resolve to eat locally and stay away from those restaurants positioning the wait staff outside their doors, calling out to you in English, and displaying plastic menus translated into multiple languages. Ask the locals or a trusted contact for recommendations.

CHICKEN PARM IS NOT ON THE MENU
You can have it here, but you won't find it there. Chicken parm is an Italian-American invention. There's no veal parmigiana either, but they do serve luscious eggplant parmigiana (*melanzane parmigiana*), the eggplant not breaded or camouflaged under a blanket of mozzarella, but bursting with the flavors of fresh tomato sauce and basil.

NEITHER ARE SPAGHETTI AND MEATBALLS

This most iconic of Italian-American dishes, spaghetti and meatballs, is considered a weird and laughable combination by the Italians who wouldn't dream of plopping *polpette* (meatballs) on top of delicate pasta. You can have those meatballs or *polpette* standing on their own as a second course, with or without tomato sauce, *after* the pasta, but never occupying the same plate.

ALFREDO IS NOT A SAUCE

So it's not on chicken, pizza, or even on fettuccine, as in fettuccine Alfredo.

In fact, fettuccine Alfredo is on the menu in Italy only at the eponymous restaurant on Via della Scrofa in Rome where it was invented in the 1920's, and where they still know how to milk a good thing. The original recipe, whipped up in the kitchen to satisfy the pregnant wife of the owner, called for fettuccine, butter, and Parmigiano-Reggiano, no heavy cream or anything else.

CAVEAT #2:
If Italians use cream at all in their pasta sauces - and it's called panna, not crema which is something else- - it's used very sparingly, so you won't encounter the popular Italian-American "pink" sauce.

ABOUT SALADS (INCLUDING CAESAR'S)

You won't find a salad hiding under chicken, salmon, or beef strips, nor will it be named Caesar, and you eat it not before dinner as we do, but at the end of the main meal where it's properly placed for digestive purposes. By this time, you've probably figured out that there's no such thing as Italian dressing either. Italians prefer a simple salad composed of tender mixed greens drizzled with extra virgin olive oil and a squeeze of fresh lemon juice or red wine vinegar, *not* balsamic. (More to follow on the proper use of balsamic)

Now about that Caesar salad:

Not Roman or even Italian at all, the classic Caesar salad (according to conventional opinion) was invented by a transplanted Italian restaurateur and chef in Tijuana, Mexico in the early 20th century. When properly made (as its creator Cesare Cardini did) with romaine, lemon juice, coddled egg, mashed garlic cloves, ground black pepper, croutons, and grated Parmigiano-Reggiano - the inclusion of anchovies is disputed - this salad, named for a mortal, would have been fit even for Julius, the god of all Caesars. Unfortunately what comes out of too many American kitchens these days is a heavy, creamy perversion of the original that should be called The Caligula, or What Mess Hath the Barbarians Wrought.

And finally about *balsamico*:

To be taken seriously in Italy, balsamic vinegar must come from Modena as the result of the same complicated method going back to the Middle Ages, be aged at least 12 and up to 50 years, and be labeled *"aceto balsamico tradizionale"*.

We Americans love to take a new idea, in this case, the trendy balsamic craze, and use it in places where no Italian would dare to go, such as over a salad. The classic uses are dripped over strawberries, chunks of Parmigiana-Reggiano, gelato (delicious!), and sparingly added to enhance meat and vegetable recipes.

TO ALL SEASONS, THERE IS A VEGETABLE

This part is biblical.

Food must be in season and it must be fresh. If it wilts, droops, comes out of a can, or from the freezer, it has no place in an Italian kitchen. Asparagus shoots up from the ground in spring and that's when you'll find it in everything from soup to gelato - really! But come autumn, you can forget about ordering *risotto con asparigi.* That's when you do as the Italians do and honor the bounties of the harvest, and enjoy the many varieties of squash stuffed into ravioli, earthy mushrooms such as *porcini* and *ovoli*, and those aphrodisiacal *tartufi (*white truffles) shaved over pasta, risotto, or veal scallops.

THINGS WE DO THAT ITALIANS DON'T

The Bread Dip: Bread is placed on the table shortly after you sit down and often at a small charge. If you're lucky, it'll be crusty, dense, and fresh from the oven. What it won't be is accompanied by olive oil and herbs or - sacre blu! - balsamic vinegar. Wherever this prelude to the meal of the olive oil bread bath began, it was not in Italy, for as anyone there knows, such a combination is much too heavy on the stomach at the beginning of a meal. (Italians don't butter their bread either.)

The Spaghetti Spoon: Unless you order soup, don't expect to be offered a large spoon. Italians twirl their spaghetti or other long pasta on the side of the plate using just the fork. Only children and those with small motor skill difficulties get the spoon for this purpose.

The Doggie Bag: Italians don't leave restaurants with bags of dinner scraps tucked under their arms. Portions are not usually large, and they seldom have anything left over on the plate anyway.

Martini Before Dinner: Italians have been winos for over 2000 years and never caught on to the idea of a cocktail before dinner, so unless you're in a large hotel restaurant with American overtones, hard liquor won't even be an option. Instead try an *aperitivo,* often taken at a bar on the way to dinner, which might be any number of low percentage alcoholic beverages such as *alperol, campari,* or my personal favorite and now gaining popularity all over the US, *prosecco.*

Coffee With Dinner: (Some of us do this!) Italy is a country of coffee addicts which may seem strange when you realize that the dominant version is less than two ounces of *espresso* in a tiny cup which they refer to as *caffe'*. The proper times and manner of drinking *un caffe'* is in the morning gulped down quickly while standing up at a bar, periodically throughout the day for a quick energy jolt (the real *tira mi su*- "pick me up"), and then at dinner after dessert. The cut-off time for having a cappuccino is about 11 a.m. There's a good reason for this. If asked, any Italian will tell you that milk should not be sitting there in your stomach waiting for the food to arrive at lunch. Nor should it be added to the mix after a meal - very bad for the digestion.

Glorifying Garlic: The biggest misconception about Italian food is that garlic rules. It doesn't. In fact, when garlic is called for in a recipe, it's used sparingly. As a Roman chef once told me, garlic should never be the protagonist in a dish. It's a supporting player, called upon when needed and considered bad form when it tries to steal the show.

SOME DIFFERENCES IN TRANSLATION

Biscotti: Biscotti is the Italian word for cookies. If you want the long, hard sweet we think of as *biscotti*, you must ask for *tozzetti* or *cantuccini*. Otherwise you might get a macaroon.

Spaghetti with clam sauce: Look for spaghetti or *linguine vongole veraci*, made with tiny clams in the shell, olive oil, a *little* garlic, parsley, peperoncino (chili pepper). It's never served with cheese, cream, basil, oregano, or angel hair pasta.

Shrimp scampi: There is no such dish. Shrimp scampi translates to "shrimp shrimp" in Italian. Among the many varieties of shrimp besides *scampi* are *gamberi, gamberetti,* and *mazzancolle*.

Scaloppine: *Scaloppine*, whether veal, pork, or chicken, is not a dish. It's a butcher's cut of meat.

Italian hoagies, submarines, grinders: Sandwiches in Italy are flat, never over-stuffed and are called *panini* or *tramezzini*.

Tomato sauce or gravy: Whatever you call it, it helps to know the two basic tomato sauces among the many regional varieties in Italy:

Ragu is a meat sauce, usually slow-cooked.

Sugo di pomodoro is a light, quickly cooked, meatless tomato sauce made from either fresh tomatoes or from canned tomatoes called *la salsa*.

(*Marinara* generally refers to *pizza alla marinara*—with tomatoes, garlic, and oregano.)

LET US NOW PRAISE PASTA
Beautiful and white
As you emerge in groups
Out of the machine.
If on a cloth
you are made to lie
You look to me like the milky way
Zounds!
Great desire,
Master of this earthly life,
I waste away,
I faint from the wish
To taste you
O maccheroni!

--Filipo Sagruttendio, Naples, 1646

THE SACRED "P"S

After all is said and done, what we all want when we go to Italy is pasta and pizza.

HOLY MACARONI!

No misconception here. Italians love their pasta which they honor in the form of festivals, museums, and poetry. Pasta takes hundreds of forms, shapes, and sizes. It can be dried, fresh, rolled, flat, filled, short or long, made with or without eggs, and with a variety of other ingredients. And each has a name, some amusing such as the elongated and twisted *strozzapreti* (priest-stranglers) common in Umbria and revealing the less than pious attitude of the locals toward members of the clergy. Others such as *farfalle* (butterflies), *capellini* (little hats), or *orecchiette* (little ears) are merely descriptive. It doesn't end there. Only particular pastas marry with certain sauces:

bucatini with *carbonara*, *fettuccine* with wild boar sauce, *trenette* with *pesto*. No mixing and matching allowed.

In addition, not every pasta dish gets topped with a grating of cheese, but when it does the kind of cheese (usually *Parmigiano-Reggiano* or *pecorino)* that tops the pasta is mandated by a sort of culinary edict. A general rule stands that cheese is never added to seafood pasta since the tastes and properties of milk and fish are oppositional, but there are exceptions when perhaps a shaved *pecorino* (sharp sheep milk cheese) will be called for. You can relax about this since the choice is not yours to make. Your waiter will let you know.

PIZZA

A national law states what may and may not be called Real Neapolitan Pizza, three criteria being the shape (round), the size (no more than 35 centimeters), and the tomatoes which must come from the lava rich soil at the foot of Mount Vesuvius. It's officially documented that pizza was born in Naples and any Neapolitan will tear the eyes right out of your head if you suggest otherwise.

That said, pizza shows up in every little burg in Italy, thickness of the crust and preferred toppings being regional. For example, Roman pizza is very thin and crispy and might be topped with potatoes, zucchini, and mozzarella or simply unadorned, such as in Rome's famous *pizza bianca*, white pizza lightly salted and brushed with olive oil. In spite of the infinite possibilities for toppings (please, no pineapple!), the *Pizza Margherita,* invented in honor of the first Queen of Italy upon her visit to Naples in 1889, is still the classic - with fresh tomatoes, mozzarella, and basil representing the colors of the Italian flag. Until very recently, really wonderful pizza was only served in the evening, after the ovens had time to become sufficiently hot. In the daytime hours, *pizza al taglio* (by the slice and usually not all that good) was available from take-out places catering to tourists hurrying from museum to monument That's changing now. With a new wave of excellent pizzerias breaking the old mold, pizza for lunch can be a sublime experience.

CAVEAT # 3
Pepperoni pizza is a vegetarian dish. Peperoni in Italy are peppers, not the round discs of cured meat we call pepperoni. Instead try sausage (salsiccia) on that pizza.

THE SEQUENCE OF THE MEAL IN ITALY

Not only is the time frame different from ours (lunch from 1 pm to 3 pm and dinner from 8 pm to 10 pm), the order of the courses is not the same either.

ANTIPASTO (Appetizers)

Don't imagine a platter of salami, mortadella, marinated artichokes, and provolone. An antipasto in Italy is so very much more. Selections again are regionally determined and next to the pasta the most interesting part of the meal.

Among the dizzying array of choices are frittatas, seafood salads, sweet and sour onions, vegetables roasted or grilled, smoked or marinated fish, or the simple and elegant prosciutto and melon or figs.

IL PRIMO (First Course)
Generally the most exciting part of the meal, *il primo* includes the dishes most widely identifiable around the world as Italian. Choose from *zuppa* (soup, thick and hearty or brothy), *risotto, polenta,* and, of course, pasta.

IL SECONDO (Second Course)
Il secondo is the protein part of the meal - fish, fowl, meat, or even grilled cheese such as *provola*. It's perfectly permissible to skip this course and go straight to the *contorno* (below) or to the cheese or dessert courses. You can also substitute an *antipasto* selection here.

IL CONTORNO (Side Dish)
Il contorno could be a vegetable or potato served along with the second course or a salad served afterward.

IL FORMAGGIO (Cheese Course)
Technically the cheese course (composed of an array of sheep, goat, and cow cheeses) comes after the second course and *contorno* and before the dessert. Today it's more commonly enjoyed, if at all, in place of dessert and given its own featured spot only at formal dinners and banquets.

I DOLCI (Dessert)

Fundamentals of Italian desserts:

1. Rich, gooey, and large enough to feed a small naval base are never part of the equation.

2. They're not overly sweet, so no sugar high follows.

3. They're often tied to historical or religious traditions.

4. Many Italians prefer a bowl of seasonal fruit which is their answer to low-fat dessert.

IL CAFFE' (Coffee)

Coffee (espresso for the Italians) comes after dessert, never before or with it. Having a cappuccino after dinner for an Italian would be a violation of their culinary code, but for a tourist - and especially an American tourist - it's perfectly acceptable.

IL DIGESTIVO (After dinner liqueur)

The grand finale! Italians frequently punctuate a long, leisurely meal with a *digestivo*, perhaps a *grappa*, a grape derivative, or an *amaro*, made from herbs and nearly in the medicinal category. Italians insist that the liqueurs aid in digestion allowing them to do this all over again the next day.

IN CONCLUSION

Ever since 46 BC when Julius Caesar held a candlelit dinner for 22,000 of his closest friends on the Palatine Hill, Italians have loved gathering around the table. They still do. The poetic soul of the Italians in every region is best expressed by the creating, the sharing, and the sheer pleasure found in this most revered of all Italian art forms, the art of eating.

So set yourself up for the culinary experience of a lifetime. Go to Italy with a *tabula rosa*, a blank slate, and allow yourself to fall in love with Italian food in the place where it all began.

ABOUT THE AUTHOR

Carol Coviello-Malzone, writer, culinary tour hostess, and travel consultant, has been traveling to Italy extensively since 1992. In the name of research, she has eaten her way through most of Italy, stopping occasionally for cooking classes, seminars, and any food or wine festival en route.

Carol is the author of *Flavors of Rome: How, What, & Where to Eat in The Eternal City* and *Best Restaurants in Rome 2010.*

To read more about her ventures, consulting options, and recipes please visit: www.flavorsofrome.com

www.ingramcontent.com/pod-product-compliance
Lightning Source LLC
Chambersburg PA
CBHW041744040426
42444CB00001B/23